DESERT ANIMALS

ISBN 0-590-40740-6

Copyright © 1987 by Ilex Publishers Limited
Illustrated by Dick Twinney / Linden Artists
All rights reserved. Published by
Scholastic Inc., 730 Broadway, New York, NY 10003
by arrangement with Ilex Publishers Limited

12 11 10 9 8 7 6 5 4 3 2 1   7 8 9/8 0 1 2/9

Printed in Italy

First Scholastic printing: April 1987

DESERT ANIMALS

Written by Mark Carwardine
Illustrated by Dick Twinney

SCHOLASTIC INC.
New York   Toronto   London   Auckland   Sydney

This series is dedicated to Georgia, aged 7 who
showed us how children look at animals

CONTENTS

Desert Animals arranged by geographical location

Jackrabbit

Jackrabbits are perfectly adapted to desert life. They have enormous movable ears, which they use as radiators to let off heat in the scorching desert sun. If the temperature drops too low, jackrabbits simply fold their ears back to stop body heat from escaping.

Their ears are also very important for detecting sounds, to warn them of approaching predators so that they can quickly dash away to safety. Like all rabbits and hares, jackrabbits are specially adapted for running and jumping. Some can reach speeds of up to fifty miles an hour and have been seen leaping over horses.

Jackrabbits live in the United States and Mexico. They feed at night, or at twilight, when it is cooler and less dangerous to move around in the open. Yucca plants and cacti — which they eat very carefully to avoid the prickly spines — are their favorite food; these plants contain so much moisture that the jackrabbits really don't need to drink if they eat enough.

Since they prefer not to sit in the sun for too long, most of the daytime is spent resting or sleeping in the shade of rocks or bushes.

Roadrunner

In the deserts of the southern United States and northern Mexico a very strange bird spends most of its time running backwards and forwards, twisting and turning in and out of the cactus thickets. Clucking and crowing as it goes, the roadrunner can easily outrun a man and often reaches speeds of up to fifteen miles an hour. It can fly — by running along like a hang glider pilot and leaping into the air — but prefers to keep its feet firmly on the ground.

The roadrunner is an expert at killing snakes and lizards. It quietly waits near rocks and stones, until one of the unsuspecting animals makes a move. Then the roadrunner chases after the animal and stabs it with its long, pointed beak.

If necessary, the roadrunner kills the prey properly by banging its head on the ground. Roadrunners also eat scorpions, tarantulas, centipedes and many other desert animals.

One of the roadrunner's favorite pastimes is grasshopper hunting. Excitedly leaping about all over the place, it goes wild trying to catch the hoppers in midair.

In fact, they are usually so busy leaping and running

bush and hope for the best. But although they belong to the cuckoo family, roadrunners do take the trouble to incubate their eggs themselves. The baby birds hatch after about two and a half weeks and begin to run around with their parents as soon as they have grown feathers.

around in the desert that they never seem to find time to build a proper nest. They simply balance a few twigs and branches in a tree or

Desert pupfish

Fish are probably the least likely animals you would expect to find living in the desert. But in parts of Arizona, southeastern California, and Mexico they are fairly common.

They live in the regions that were once great lakes but are now deserts. A few springs, pools and small creeks were left behind when the lakes disappeared and the fish, known as desert pupfish, were left behind with them. The water in these places is usually less than three feet deep and fairly cool.

DICK TWINNEY

But the pupfish also live in hot springs where the water temperatures can be as high as 122°F in the middle of the day.

There is another similar and closely related fish, the Devil's Hole pupfish, which lives in a small part of a spring-fed pool in Nevada. The pool is about fifty feet below the desert floor and is only ten feet by fifty feet in size. The fish are therefore trapped in the middle of an otherwise waterless desert with no means of escape.

Desert tortoise

It would take a desert tortoise over an hour to walk a city block. Like all tortoises, it moves very slowly because it has to carry its enormous shell wherever it goes.

Found in parts of the United States and Mexico, desert tortoises live in deserts with plenty of scrub. They feed on the most juicy plants and, unlike many other desert animals, like to drink water whenever they can.

They live for about fifty years or more in the wild. They do not start breeding until they are at least fifteen years old. Courtship in tortoises often involves a lot of head-butting, during which the females are butted and bitten by the males. They lay hard, round eggs, which hatch after several months. The baby tortoises grow almost half an inch every year. They grow fastest between April and July, or after heavy rains.

Desert tortoises are now quite rare. This is partly because they used to be very popular as pets and enormous numbers were taken from the wild to be sold in pet shops. Now it is against the law to collect them.

There are forty-one different kinds of tortoises living in many parts of the world. They are especially common in the tropics and subtropics.

Rattlesnake

In the dry, rocky deserts of America lives a rather evil-looking snake with a very bad reputation. Its frightening rattle can be heard a hundred feet away, and it can strike with lightning speed.

But the rattlesnake, or "rattler" as it's sometimes called, prefers to avoid people if it possibly can. It holds its tail upright and rattles the end whenever it is disturbed, in the hope that the intruder will go away. However, if its warnings are ignored — and it feels threatened — it will coil, ready to bite.

But the rattler itself cannot hear the noise its tail makes. Like most snakes, it "hears" things through vibrations in the ground. If a person walks nearby, the snake can feel the movement. But if the same person were to shout, it would not hear a thing.

Rattlesnakes are very common and widespread animals, living right across the American continent from Canada to Argentina. They feed on a variety of prey, including mice, voles, rats, chipmunks and many other small animals. Young rattlers are born alive and can be up to a third of the length of their parents.

Scorpion

Scorpions are probably the least popular of all desert animals. Although they are common in most deserts, they like to hide under rocks and stones and are rarely seen.

They come out at night, when the sun has gone down and the desert is cooler, to hunt for beetles, cockroaches and other small animals. The size of the prey depends on the size of the scorpion, which can range anywhere from less than half an inch to well over seven inches in length.

Once it has caught an animal, the scorpion stings it with the needle on the end of its tail. This sting is also used in self-defense. It feels like a very fast and painful

injection but, in most cases, is no more serious than a bee sting. Some of the six hundred different scorpions known in the world, however, are deadly. The poison of the Sahara scorpion is as strong as the venom of a cobra and can kill a dog within a few seconds.

Scorpions are related to spiders. Like their long-legged relatives, they often have very impressive courtship displays. The male holds his mate's pincers and walks her round and round in circles, in what is known as the "scorpion's dance."

The female lays eggs, but they hatch almost immediately into miniature scorpions — just like smaller versions of their parents. The babies climb onto their mother's back and she carries them around wherever she goes until they are old enough to take care of themselves.

Elf owl

Visitors to deserts of the southwestern United States and eastern Mexico might well think that the giant cactus plants there make strange noises. Rapidly-repeated, high-pitched cackles can often be heard coming from inside holes in the cacti.

The sounds are being made by the elf owl, an animal no bigger than a sparrow and one of the smallest owls in the world. Its call is extremely loud and sounds as if it should be coming from a much larger animal.

Elf owls live in many different places, from woodlands and forests to grasslands. But they prefer living in the desert because they can use the giant cacti for nesting and roosting. They live in the holes pecked out by woodpeckers and other birds. Normally, the owl lives in the hole by day and moves out for its nightly hunt when the woodpecker comes home to roost before dusk. But sometimes the owls are so eager that they move in to nest even before the rightful owners have moved out.

The female owl lays up to five pure white eggs in the cactus. She shares incubation with her mate until the eggs hatch, some two weeks later.

Both parents feed the owlets together, mostly on animals which live on or very near the ground, such as crickets, cicadas, beetles, moths and other large insects.

Hairy armadillo

Hairy armadillos dig into the ground so quickly that they seem to vanish before your eyes. They have to be fast because they hold their breath when digging, to make sure they don't breathe in all the dust.

"Armadillo" actually means "little armored one." It is a fitting name because armadillos are covered in armor plating, which protects them from thorns and branches, and from their enemies. Hairy armadillos, which live in the deserts of southern South America, are so-called because their armor is sparsely covered with brown hairs.

DICK TWINNEY

Armadillos are night animals. They leave the safety of their underground homes after dark, to search for ants and termites, which are their favorite food. They push their long, worm-shaped tongues into the insects' nests and often stay there eating all day. They also feed on many other kinds of animals and plants and have been seen killing small snakes, by throwing themselves onto the unsuspecting animals and cutting them with the edges of their shells.

The hairy armadillos alive today are usually about twenty inches long from the tip of the nose to the end of the tail. But some armadillos — kinds which unfortunately are now extinct — were more than six times that length. Their armored shells were so enormous that they were used as roofs by the early South American Indians.

Ostrich

Ostriches are the largest birds in the world. Found in many parts of Africa, they have been known to grow to nearly ten feet tall.

Because they are so enormous they are unable to fly. Instead, they walk and run everywhere, sometimes reaching speeds of over thirty miles per hour.

Ostriches eat shoots, leaves, flowers and seeds. While feeding, they often raise their heads to scan the landscape for lions, leopards and cheetahs. It would be very dangerous for an ostrich to keep its head down in the vegetation too long, because it wouldn't know if a predator was approaching. Perhaps for the same reason — and despite all the sayings — ostriches never bury their heads in the sand.

DICK TWINNEY

Because they are such large birds, they lay enormous eggs. The male, which is black with white patches on its wings, makes a nest on the ground for the brown female to lay her eggs. Then several other females come along and also lay their eggs in the same nest!

The first female incubates the eggs by day and the male incubates them by night. They also have to guard the eggs from vultures, hyenas and jackals. When the eggs hatch, all the chicks from several nests are looked after together by one or two adults, until they are old enough to take care of themselves.

Banded mongoose

Poking their noses into holes, overturning rocks with their paws and scratching the ground with their sharp claws, banded mongooses are very amusing animals to watch. A common sight in many parts of Africa, they travel in groups of about twenty to forage for beetles, millipedes and other small and tasty creatures.

They like to hunt together, keeping in touch whenever they go out of sight behind rocks or bushes by twittering and calling. Always on the lookout for danger — hawks, eagles and large snakes — they warn one another with a special alarm call if they spot anything suspicious.

DICK TWINNEY

Mongooses are famous for being able to kill snakes without getting hurt themselves. Their reactions are so fast that they can dodge each time the snake strikes. After a while, when the snake gets tired of fighting, the mongoose quickly dives in for the kill.

All the females have their kittens at about the same time. They are raised by the whole group in a den made inside an old termite mound or hollow log. When most of the adults are out looking for food, one or two males stay behind to stand guard until the others return for the night.

Camel

A thirsty camel can drink as much as thirty gallons of water — that's about five hundred full glasses — in just ten minutes. Normally, however, it gets all the moisture it needs from desert plants and can survive for up to ten months without drinking any water at all.

There are two different kinds of camels. One, known as the dromedary, has only a single hump; the other is called a bactrian camel and has two humps. The humps help camels survive in the desert by acting as storage containers. But the humps don't store water, as many people falsely believe. Instead, they are full of fat. This fat nourishes the camels when food is scarce. If

camels have nothing to eat for several days, their humps shrink as the fat is used up.

There are many other ways in which camels are adapted to desert life. Their mouths are so tough that even sharp thorns of desert plants don't hurt them; they can survive much higher temperatures than most other animals; and they even have bushy eyebrows and a double row of eyelashes, to keep out the desert sand.

There are many millions of camels throughout the world. But they have nearly all been domesticated, or tamed, by man. There are now probably fewer than a thousand left roaming in the wild.

Desert jerboa

The desert jerboa is an expert jumper. It can easily cover more than nine feet in a single bound. Its enormous back legs, which are four times longer than its front legs, enable the animal to spring like a miniature kangaroo. When it is in midair, it uses its long tail for balance.

Desert jerboas live in long underground burrows with many passages and chambers. They dig these themselves, using their short front feet and teeth for digging and their long back legs for throwing away the sand. Usually, there is one jerboa to a burrow. But they are friendly animals and sometimes allow two or three others to share their nests.

In the spring and summer, jerboas often plug up their burrows from the inside during the day, or from the outside after leaving at night. This helps keep out the tremendous desert heat. But jerboas always have special emergency exits — just in case a predator gets inside — through which they can burst back into the desert. Then they can quickly leap away to safety.

Unless they are in a hurry, jerboas move slowly, either walking on their hind legs or hopping around like rabbits. Their feet are furry on the bottom to stop them from sinking in the soft sand.

Desert jerboas feed on beetles and other insects, seeds and plants.

Sandgrouse

Sandgrouse spend most of their time eating and sleeping. They feed all day on small seeds and then sleep all night. Sometimes they eat more than a thousand seeds in just a few hours, stopping only to rest in the shade of a bush during the hottest part of the day.

Even the chicks, which look a bit like pigeons, feed on small seeds within a few hours of hatching. Their mothers teach them how to peck.

Sandgrouse need to drink every couple of days. Large flocks of hundreds or thousands of them gather at the main water holes. Sometimes they fly over ninety miles round trip to a water hole.

Young sandgrouse also need water, but they are unable to get it themselves. So the males bring the water to them. They wade into the water hole up to their bellies and wait until their feathers are soaking wet. Then they

DICKTWINNEY
86

fly back to their chicks and, when the young birds have drunk enough, walk away and dry their feathers on a patch of sand.

But, water holes are dangerous places. When they arrive, the sandgrouse have to check that there are no falcons, foxes, jackals or mongooses hiding nearby. If they sense danger, they may crouch on the ground to avoid being seen, or they make a quick getaway on their long, pointed wings.

Sooty falcon

Some animals live in the desert for only part of their lives. The sooty falcon, for example, breeds in the deserts of north Africa but flies south every autumn to spend its winter in the completely different surroundings of Madagascar.

During the summer months in the desert, sooty falcons feed on small birds. They lie in wait for migrating birds that come down to bushes and trees for a rest after their long journeys from Europe. Tired and hungry, these birds are easy to catch.

The falcons usually wait until late in the summer to breed, when the chicks of most other birds have already left home. Their eggs are laid in August, carefully timed to hatch in the middle of the migrating season.

At this time of year, there are more small birds for the parents to catch for their chicks.

As soon as the chicks are ready to leave their nests, the falcons begin their own migrations. They stop catching small birds and begin to eat insects instead. They do this all winter in Madagascar and don't eat birds until about six months later, when they return to the deserts once again.

DICK TWINNEY

33

Houbara bustard

In parts of north Africa, the Middle East and Asia, a strange-looking bird spends its days wandering over the dry, open deserts. Although it has long legs and a long neck, it is difficult to see against the stony desert background and is too nervous to approach very closely.

Known as the houbara bustard, it wanders around in search of small animals and tasty plants to eat. "Bustard" actually means "the bird that walks." The houbara certainly spends a great deal of time on its feet, even though it is able to fly. Indeed, it is one of the largest flying birds in the world.

Sadly, the houbara bustard is becoming quite scarce because of hunting.

Thousands are killed every year, and the animal has been wiped out from many parts of its range. The hunters use rare and beautiful falcons to kill the bustards for fun.

The male houbara has a spectacular courtship display to attract females. He raises his white neck-ruff right over his head and trots around to show it off. But the ruff covers his eyes, and he is completely unable to see where he is going.

35

Gerbil

Most people know gerbils as the small, frisky pets that are so popular in many parts of the world. But there are also about a hundred kinds of wild gerbils living in the desert regions of Africa and Asia.

Desert gerbils spend the day in their cool underground burrows but come out at night to feed. The seeds, leaves, roots, flowers and insects that they eat supply them with all the water they need. They also like to gnaw on harder kinds of food because their teeth never stop growing, and they have to file them down constantly.

Gerbils are well-camouflaged little animals. Their sandy-brown fur blends in perfectly with the desert surroundings.

DICK TWINNEY
86

When they sit still, they are extremely difficult to see. But if they do get spotted, they can use their powerful kangaroo-like back legs to leap away to safety. In the middle of a jump, their tails act as rudders, enabling them to change direction in midair.

Gerbils nest inside their underground burrows. They usually have up to eight young in each litter — and several litters a year. The babies stay underground for about three weeks before beginning to search for food on their own.

Fennec fox

The ears of a fennec fox are so big that they are half as long as its body. They enable the fox to hear insects and the other small animals it eats running around at night.

Found in the Arabian desert and parts of north Africa, the fennec is the smallest wild dog in the world. It is only about twelve inches long from the tip of its nose to the end of its body. A very agile animal, it has furry feet to help it run around in the soft sand.

They are nocturnal animals, emerging to hunt in the cool of the early morning, evening or night. They eat insects, small desert mice, birds, lizards and plants. But like many desert creatures, they are able to obtain all the moisture they need from their food, so they rarely, if ever, need to drink.

NICK TWINNEY
'86

Fennec foxes live in small groups in long tunnels under the desert. They dig these tunnels themselves — sometimes so rapidly that they appear to be sinking into the ground.

Arabian oryx

The Arabian oryx became extinct in the wild in 1972. Although once common throughout Arabia, up through Jordan and into Syria and Iraq, they were wiped out by hunters in less than thirty years. Facing hunters with fast cars and automatic rifles, these beautiful animals did not stand a chance.

Fortunately, however, a few oryx had been taken to zoos in Arabia and the United States before they could be killed. These were carefully bred and now there are enough to attempt to establish them in the wild once again. Hunting is no longer allowed and a small herd has already been released in Oman, so perhaps one day they will be back living wild and free in all their old haunts.

Arabian oryx live in small herds. Unlike many other animals, they rarely fight and happily share their food and the shade of a tree with other members of the group.

They spend most of the day sheltering together from the scorching sun. When it gets cooler, towards the end of the afternoon, they begin to spread out and start feeding. But they look up regularly to search for enemies and to make sure that no members of the herd are missing.

Przewalski's horse

In the cold deserts of
Mongolia lives the rarest
horse in the world. Known as
the Przewalski's horse, and
named after a famous
Russian explorer, it has been
hunted almost to extinction.

There are about two hundred of them living in zoos in various parts of the world. But no one knows how many are still surviving in the wild. One was seen in 1968 but, despite a great deal of searching, none has been spotted since. It is even possible that this ancestor of our domestic horse, which once roamed in many parts of Asia, has already become extinct.

About the same size as a domestic horse, the Przewalski's used to live in small herds, consisting of one male, called a stallion, and a few females, the mares. Like all horses, they have been admired by man for centuries for their strength, beauty, spirit and speed. They feed on grass and other plants, which they bite off with their front teeth. Then they grind the food with their large, ridged back teeth before swallowing.

A single foal is born, usually every other year. It is up and around within an hour of birth and begins grazing with its parents when just a few weeks old.

Australian frilled lizard

Most lizards run away or hide when they are frightened or under attack. But the Australian frilled lizard stands firm and tries to scare its enemies away. It opens out a gigantic flap of loose skin, called a "ruff," behind its head and inflates its body. This makes it look much bigger — and much more dangerous — than it actually is. Then it makes horrible and furious hissing sounds like a snake.

Normally, the sight of a frilled lizard in action is enough to frighten even the boldest and biggest of its enemies. But if the enemy isn't scared by the ruff — which can be as long as twelve inches across — the lizard desperately runs away on its back legs.

Frilled lizards are also able to climb trees. They often leave the desert floor in their constant search for insects, spiders and other small animals suitable for eating.

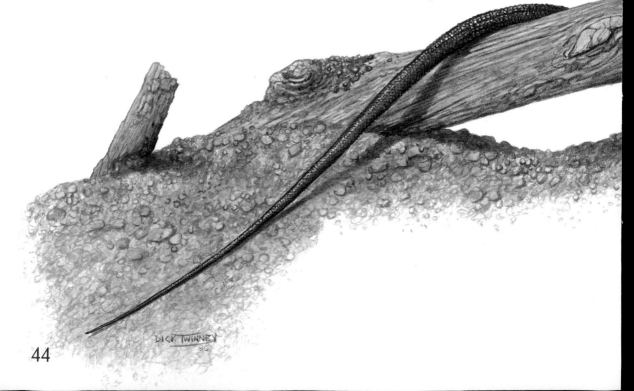

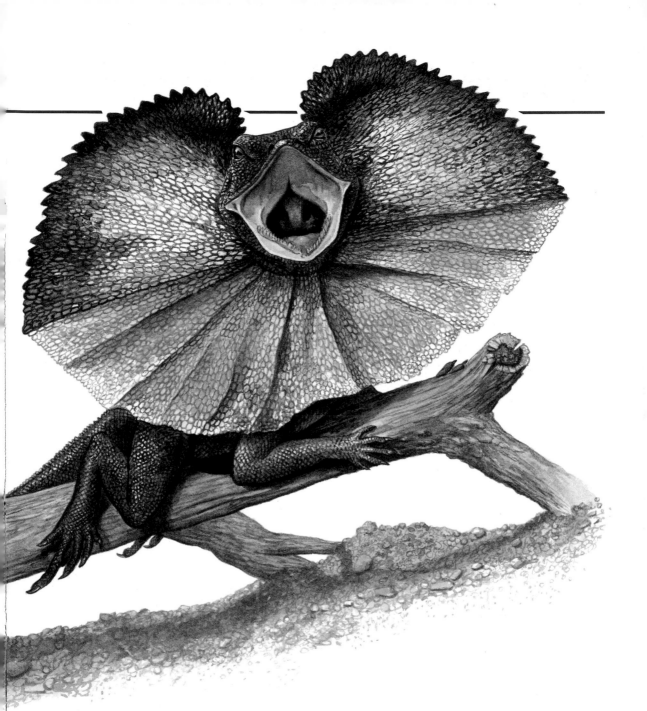

Found in northern Australia and New Guinea, they can grow to be more than thirty inches long. They usually keep their ruffs folded back against their bodies, almost out of sight, unless an enemy comes nearby. But they also use them for courtship, as a spectacular display to impress potential mates.

45